Sophie & The Italian Magician

At The Fair

One day Sophie went to a fair with her parents and they saw an Italian magician.

The magician greeted everyone with **ciao**. Italians say hi by saying **ciao**. Then he said in Italian that his name was Luca.

For his first trick, the Italian magician put three boxes on a table. He placed a coin in one of the boxes. He then told everyone to clap and count to three in Italian. And if you are reading this story now then please join in too as the magician needs as much help as possible:

uno   due   tre

Then they all had to guess which box the coin was in!

Sophie watched in amazement. It wasn't in **uno**. It wasn't in **due**. And it *wasn't* in **tre**!

The coin had disappeared!

For his next trick, he asked everyone to clap and say three times **un coniglio**.

Sophie's mum whispered to her that **un coniglio** was the Italian word for a rabbit. And then suddenly out of his hat came…….

un coniglio

Next the Italian magician got out his wand. He told everyone to clap and say three times **un uccello**.

Sophie's mum whispered to her that **un uccello** was the Italian word for a bird.

Suddenly **un uccello** appeared on the table!

How had he done that? It was amazing!

Next he turned to Sophie and he asked:

> Qual è il tuo animale preferito?

> Il cane.

Sophie realised that **animale preferito** meant favourite animal. So she replied **il cane** as she liked dogs. Surely he couldn't make **un cane** appear! This time, he had a very long balloon in his hand. He asked the crowd to join in with him as he said:

> Un cane   un cane   U N C A N E.

And then suddenly the balloon turned into….

un cane

It had been so much fun watching the Italian magician! For his final trick he placed his hat on the floor and he asked everyone to say **caramelle** three times as they clapped:

Caramelle caramelle caramelle.

And out of the hat came **delle caramelle** - lots and lots of delicious looking sweets! That was really amazing! Everyone thanked the Italian magician by saying "**grazie**".

That was the Italian magician's last trick, so they all said "**ciao**" and waved goodbye.

Sophie & The Italian Magician

Sophie's Birthday Party

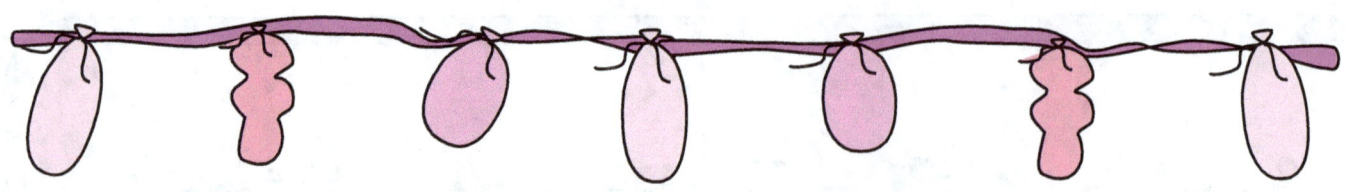

It was Sophie's birthday, and the Italian magician arrived at her birthday party!

Ciao,
Mi chiamo Luca.

The Italian magician said hello in Italian. Then he said that his name was Luca.

Sophie introduced herself in Italian to the Italian magician.

Ciao,
Mi chiamo Sophie.

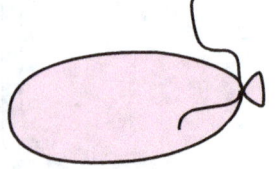
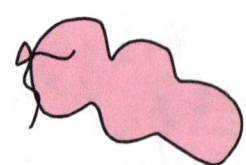
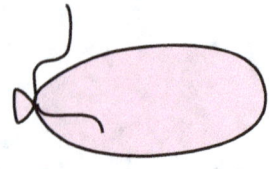

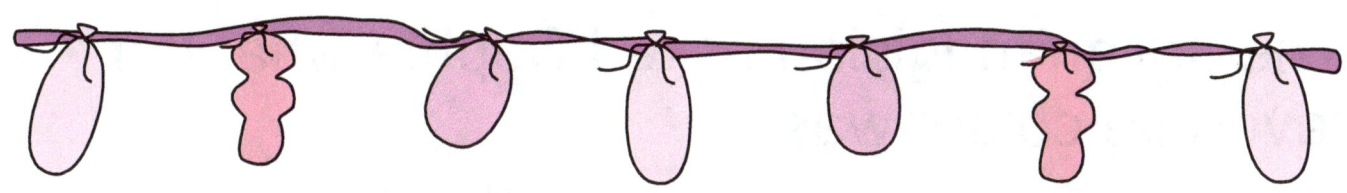

The Italian magician asked Sophie how she was:

Come stai?

Sophie was feeling **very good** as it was her birthday party! So she replied:

Molto bene.

The Italian magician asked Sophie what her favourite colour was.

Sophie's favourite colour was pink, so she said **rosa.** Pink in Italian is **rosa**.

Okay, boys and girls I need your help!
We need to say **rosa** three times as we clap.

(Now the magician needs as much help as possible, so if you're reading this story now, please join in too!)

Rosa   rosa   rosa.

And out of the hat came a teddy that was the colour….

Sophie was so happy that she thanked the magician in Italian.

Next the magician turned to Sophie's best friend, and he asked:

Qual'è il tuo colore preferito?

Blu.

Sophie's best friend said blue was her favourite colour.

Okay, boys and girls I need your help!
We need to say **blu** three times as we clap.

(Now the magician needs as much help as possible, so if you're reading this story now, please join in too!)

Blu   blu   blu.

And out of the hat came a teddy that was the colour….

blu

Sophie's best friend was so happy that she thanked the magician in Italian.

Next the Italian magician asked a boy:

The boy said green was his favourite colour.

Okay, boys and girls I need your help!
We need to say **verde** three times as we clap.

(Now the magician needs as much help as possible, so if you're reading this story now, please join in too!)

Verde   verde   verde.

And out of the hat came a teddy that was the colour….

Wow, what a magician!

Out of the hat kept on coming more and more teddies for Sophie's friends!

Eventually EVERYONE had a new teddy!

Can you remember the colours in Italian for all the new teddies? Lets say them together!

It had been a wonderful birthday party! The Italian magician waved goodbye and they all said "**Ciao**."

© Joanne Leyland   2023

The useful Italian words and phrases and the song lyrics may be photocopied by the purchasing individual or institution for use in class or at home. The rest of the book may not be photocopied or reproduced digitally without the prior written agreement of the author.

Useful Italian words and phrases

Ciao …………………………………… Hi / Bye
Mi chiamo ………………………….. My name is …
Come stai? …………………………… How are you?
Molto bene ………………………. Very well
Grazie ………………………………… Thank you

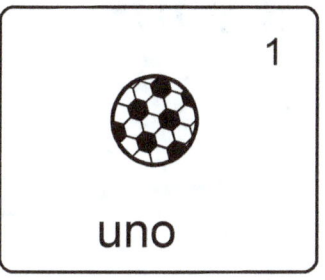 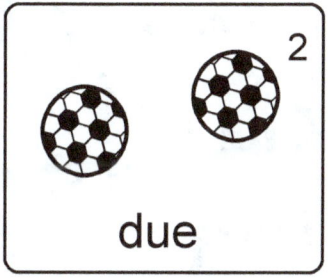 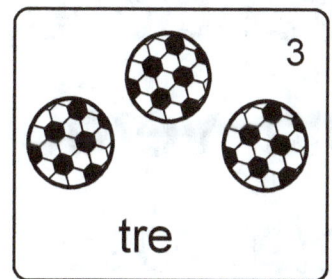 

uno — due — tre — caramelle (sweets)

Qual è il tuo animale preferito?….. What is your favourite animal?

il coniglio - the rabbit / un coniglio - a rabbit
l'uccello - the bird / un uccello - a bird
il cane - the dog / un cane - a dog

Qual è il tuo colore preferito?….. What is your favourite colour?

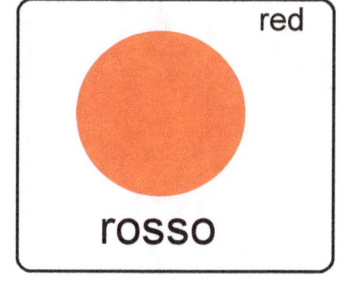 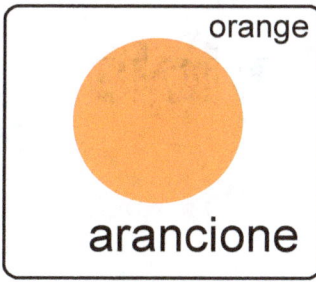 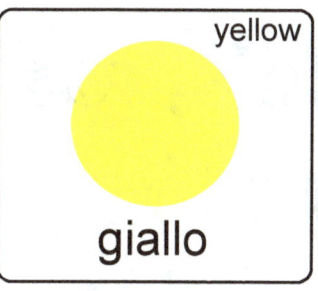 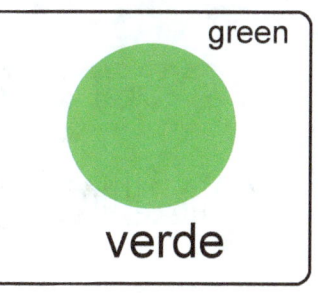

rosso (red) — arancione (orange) — giallo (yellow) — verde (green)

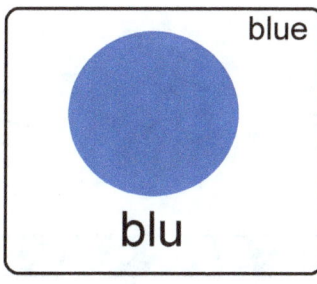 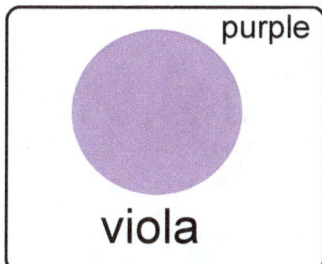 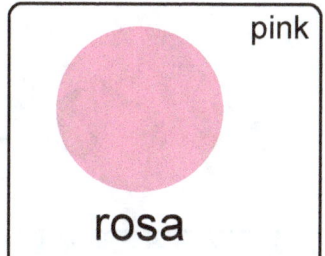

blu (blue) — viola (purple) — rosa (pink)

© Joanne Leyland - This page may be photocopied by the purchasing individual or institution for use in class or at home

Let's sing a song!

The following words could either be sung to a made up tune, or you could try saying the words as a rap.

For inspiration of a melody to use you could hum first a nursery rhyme. How many different versions can you create using the lyrics?

rosso arancione, rosso arancione
verde blu, verde blu
rosa viola, rosa viola
giallo, giallo

rosso arancione, rosso arancione
verde blu, verde blu
rosa viola, rosa viola
giallo, giallo

© Joanne Leyland - This page may be photocopied by the purchasing individual or institution for use in class or at home

www.ingramcontent.com/pod-product-compliance
Lightning Source LLC
Chambersburg PA
CBHW081629100526
44590CB00021B/3667